Sexual Healing

By Judith V. Peart

Sexual Healing Copyright 2001 by Judith Peart

All rights reserved. No part of this book may be reproduced in any form, except for the inclusion of brief quotations in a review, without permission in writing from the author.

ISBN: 978-1-304-54034-8

References

All scriptures are quoted from the King James, unless otherwise noted. All underscoring, parenthetical notes, brackets, bold lettering, literal definitions of the Scriptures in this text are supplied by this author. They are supplied for emphasis and clarity. All single quotes within the Scriptures are the literal Greek definitions inserted by this author for clarity. All "thee," "thine," "ye," "thou" words ending in "th," "lt," and so on are replaced with the appropriate modern renditions for easy reading.

Hebrew and Greek Definitions:
Strong's Exhaustive Concordance
Vines Expository Dictionary
BibleWorks Software

Table of Contents

Dedication	i
Acknowledgement	iii
Foreword	v
Introduction	1
Poem:"Freedom"	3
Testimonies: Out in the Open	5
Lesson #1: Secret Sins are Generational	21
Lesson #2: Healing Offences	27
Prophetic Word: The God That Causes All Things to Be	35
Lesson #3: Out of the Depths we Cry	37
Lesson #4: Humility and Forgiveness	45
Lesson #5: The Last will be First	49
Lesson #6: The Throne of His Glory	57

Dedication

I would like to dedicate this book to my daughter Charity and my four sons Donald Jr., Jeshua, Benjamin, and Jesse. Keep yourselves pure in your generation for your generation and may your Godly purity become your inner glory.

I would like to dedicate this book to every one of my family members who can identify with my past pain and defilement. I pray that God would heal you deep within of your hidden sexual sins.

I dedicate this book to every child in my past childhood, and every teenager in my teen years that I have ever defiled sexually. I ask you to please find it in your heart to forgive me. I pray that my past molestations and defilements have not transferred to caused you to become a defiler. I pray that my past wounds and dysfunctions may never cause you to wound others.

I dedicate this book to every man, woman, and child in this generation and the generations to come who long for sexual healing. May the pages of this book touch you and may the lessons taught therein enlighten your path to sexual wholeness.

Love,
Judith V. Peart

Acknowledgement

I would like to thank God the Father and the Lord Jesus Christ. I was in the process of writing this book for several years. I could not seem to assemble it, however, the Holy Spirit in his great wisdom revealed to me how I was to collect the scattered parts and compile the book you now have. Thanks Lord for everything.

I would like to thank my husband for his loving support, understanding, and encouragement in my healing process. Thank you for your determination to see me whole. Thanks for allowing me to fulfill what God has intended for me to be. You are my best friend, my lover, and my partner in this grace wherein we stand.

I would like to thank my mentor Bishop Sandra Hayden for being a pattern for me to follow from the beginning of my salvation. First impressions are lasting ones and what your life has impressed in me will be with me throughout eternity. For your continual love, counsel, support, comfort, and friendship I will always be grateful. My good friend, now it is your turn.

I would like to thank our local Church. You are my joy and rejoicing. I will always be reminded of your continual love and faith that you have for the Lord Jesus and for me. I thank you for your loving support through out the years. I can be all that I can be and it is because of you all. A Special Thanks to my spiritual daughter, Valencia Perkins, for editing the text for me. Daughter you are much appreciated.

Finally, I would like to thank all my spiritual Mothers, women of virtue, who were also influential in my ability to complete this book. Much thanks to my Aunt, Prophetess Marie Howard, my Mother-In-Law Mom Peart, Pastor Ola Buie and Pastor Lula Simon. I thank you all for your motherly love, strong counsel, and encouragement throughout the years.

Foreword

Your hearts will be touched, your feelings, and emotions challenged as you read this book of truth and love. Judith, out of a heart of love has shed light on the deception, and bondages of past sins in our lives, as an example of the healing power and love of our heavenly Father; as we too yield to the spirit of God, we too can take courage to be healed, delivered and set free.

Thank you Judith for your courage and transparency to help others as the Holy Spirit has helped you. Freely you have received. Freely you have given.

Dr. Sandra Phillips Hayden
Word Alive! Worship Center
Baltimore, MD

Introduction

Sexuality is a valuable matter with God. God has placed so much value on sexuality that men pay for it (i.e. buy it from strumpets). God also teaches that a person who gives up sex for free is worse than a harlot.

If sex is so valuable, and it is, that men pay money for it; then a woman should see her value and save her body for her husband. If God says that a woman who gives up sex for free is worse than a prostitute, then a woman should keep herself and her worth for her husband.

The man also has a tool that is meant to be an implement of covenant, and has misused the gift of God. The Hebrew word for covenant means to cut the flesh into two pieces where the blood flows, and to pass between the two pieces of flesh. Sex between husband and wife is intended to be a time of cutting covenant.

Men have abused this severely in that they have cut covenants outside of wedlock, and even in marriage, they have cut unclean covenants with other women. We label it adultery. Men ought to love their own wives and not lust after or defile another's wife or daughter.

Men should also keep their tools that were meant to procreate a Godly seed for their wives. The reason for marriage according to the Scripture is to raise up a Godly seed. Men have abused this and have brought up children outside the clean covenant of marriage.

Time does not permit me to discuss the full scale of sexuality. My wife and I, through much communication decided to allow the testimonies of this book to be written in the hope that her openness will cause many others who are trapped in sexual guilt to be freed. Hence, the subsequent lessons are intended to bring understanding, healing, and deliverance to the abused in body and heart.

May this book refresh your spirit to the reality of the power of the blood of Jesus bringing repentance (a change of the mind) through forgiveness!

Yours truly,
Donald A. Peart, called to be a son

Poem:"Freedom"

A breath of fresh air the birds fly above
A crisp breeze in nature's glory,
The sun shines as the glistening waters flow
The fish beneath as the corals grow
Refreshing as the sea,
The rains fall as the grounds flood
It's a reminder of the flow of his love,
For freedom Christ has set us free
You can be free only if you want to be.

By Judith V. Peart

Testimonies: Out in the Open

Mark 4:22, NIV: For whatever is hidden is meant to be disclosed, and whatever is concealed is meant to be brought out into the open.

This scripture was a perfect selection to help me describe the testimonies at hand. In this lesson, I mainly wanted to focus on what was brought out into the open. As you continue to read you will understand why it was brought out into the open.

Many of us know that sins that are hidden will eventually be brought to light some how, some way, and at some point in our lives.

We also know things have a beginning and those principle things are taught through bad and good experiences in our lives. We understand that a child has no power over occurrences that they have no control over. Nor, did they anticipate such occurrences in their early years.

Those early years should have been protected by their parents or loves ones, but sadly enough they were not. Many times the ones they loved and trusted betrayed that trust in one-way or another.

The child becomes a victim of an abuse that should have never taken place, and a love manipulated is a love disgraced. The child I am about to describe is I, but the fact 1s that there are so many other victims of sexual abuse that it would be impossible for authorities to report them all.

When I gave my life to Jesus Christ sixteen years ago, that was my turning point and the beginning of my healing. But, before we go into the instruction of the scriptures in the following lessons or the methods God used to heal me, I want to share some of my past and another personal testimony from a woman I lead to Christ whom God brought out of sexual abuse. Then you will see as I teach the scriptures how Jesus brought it out into the open in my life and healed me; and if you believe in Him, He will free you also.

Childhood

I was a "normal" little girl until the death of my mother at the age of four years old. I do not remember a great deal about her. However, I was told some things at a young age but they were very slight. I was desperately in need of love and there were many adults and children who were willing to give me that loved in a perverted form. My father raised me the best way he knew how, but had no prior knowledge that I was being victimized. My dad worked several jobs and was an excellent provider. Although he provided well, he could not protect well, because he was not always around many times to shield me. So what was going on?

I remember many perverted incidents that drove me to become a much-defiled teenager in need of deliverance and inner healing.

The first recalled incident

The first incident I can recall took place in a dark room while I slept over my girl friend's house at the age of six. We both went to Catholic school together; and she asked if I could stay the night. That night we both slept in the same bed and all I can remember is the fondling that took place.

That event disturbed my spirit so badly that it made me wonder if I was a girl that preferred other girls. I suppressed that thought through out my life and just continued as a "normal" child.

Boyfriends

After that occurrence time had passed and now I was in elementary school. In school, girls talked to boys all the time and of course I wondered about them. After the situation with the girl I just described above, I had a habit of taking my imagination a little too far. I was always curious about sexual things. I did not know at the time that spirits of sexual perversion ran heavy on both sides of my family. I believe that generational influences of perversion, the school girl's defilement, and the curiosity for boys led me into a deep pit that only God could deliver me out of.

Neighborhood boys started touching me, but I did not become sexually active with them at that time. The touchy feely kind of stuff lasted until I was about seventeen years old. The boys were not only boys in the neighborhood, but the defilement had later become a family thing. I can recall childhood incest with several of my relatives. I was not just a victim to sexual abuse, but also became prey to drugs and alcohol.

Drugs and Alcohol

This evil voice said, "You are defiled you are no longer worth anything, you might as well play along with them, after all it is only a game one day it will stop." It never did stop, and it never would have stopped had not Jesus intervened in my life. I am sure I would have been dead or a dying whore by now. I probably would have killed myself, but I did not have the fortitude to do it. So drugs and alcohol became a frequent outlet and an avenue to plunge even deeper into a variety of sexual sins. I drank until I was drunk many times, and marijuana usually accompanied the alcohol.

By the time I was eighteen and in college, the alcohol drinking was even heavier and cocaine started to take the place of marijuana. The drugs were Satan's plan to totally eradicate, deceive, and weaken me causing me to become subject and open to anything and everything. His next step was to resurrect my past feelings about the little girl's defilement, use my family's past promiscuous influences, and initiate me into the addiction of pornography.

Pornography

There are many people who may feel that viewing sullied movies is normal. The truth is that it is an open door for demons to lodge in your heart. I was a victim of sexual abuse, incest, attempted rape, and many other things. These things lead me to become curious to the world of pornography. It is a world of deathly pleasure. The Bible states, that "there is a way that seems right unto a man, but the end thereof is the ways of death" (Proverb 16:25).

The Bible states that the adulterous woman's house (the house of her body) is "the gate way to hell." (Proverb 7:27) Sexual perversion will take you to hell faster than any other sin. I was on that roller coaster and was headed there fast especially when I decided to test the waters.

Testing the waters

Pornography, my family, my friends, and neighbors had defiled and violated me and now I was angry. All I wanted was affection untainted and love undefiled. I longed for my mother's touch which I am sure I had as a baby and always longed for it. Now I was faced with another violator this time it was a woman. She made several attempts in our school shower room and I just ignored them. This day I could not fight her off any longer and her defilement began, but ended quickly as I loathed the whole idea of testing these new waters.

In and Out

After the encounter with the woman in school, I strongly considered an alternate life style; however, I was totally ashamed of the whole idea and felt that it was not normal. I knew that anything that makes you feel that bad could not be right. I hated the thought and the feelings, but could not fight the fantasy from all the pornography. My body began to burn like the Bible stated in the book of Romans, that homosexual's burn in their lust one towards another, and are turned over to lust after the same sex which is a judgment from God (Romans 1:27).

I was being judged and did not know it. God turned me over because of my love for pleasure, my lust overrode my hate of being defiled. Now, I was getting in too deep. I finally trampled in and out of several bisexual situations. The deeper I had gotten involved the more I despised it and the more I fought with my defilers afterwards. I hated myself and was a prisoner to the spirit of lust and perversion, so I drank away the pain and sought for a way out.

Marriage and God

I met my husband when I was fifteen years old. He was also a teenager at that time. He was a good friend of my older sister and brother. When we met we dated some, however, at the time my father felt that he was a little too old for me and suggested we wait until I graduated from high school. The separation lasted for about a year. I fell deeply in love with him and asked God to bless me with him again.

It was my prom time and he was in the Marines at the time. I asked his brother when he would be coming home from his duty station. He told me, and I sought to ask him to my prom. He accepted and after prom night we drew closer together and by the next year we were engaged.

We both gave our lives over to Jesus Christ within two weeks of one another. While joining in marriage, I asked God while crying and walking down the isle to purify me and make me a virgin again within my spirit.

About a year had passed and one night I had a dream. In that dream there was a married couple discussing their marriage. The husband said to the wife our marriage cannot be built on lies. God spoke to me in that dream and my husband interpreted the dream. He said that God does not want our marriage to be built on lies.

I confessed everything to my husband because the Bible states, "confess your faults one toward another that you may be healed." (James 5:16) I told him about the sexual sins in my past life and with whom, and he did the same. Truth brings trust and he indicated to me that because I had opened up to him, it had built a greater trust in him for me. He also expressed his commitment to protect me as my husband from any possible situations until I was totally healed, delivered, and could deflect any advances on my own. It was through Jesus Christ and my husband's willingness to treat me like a lady that helped heal my childhood hurts and defilements. We are faithful to each other and are happily married, and have been for the past sixteen years. Together God has blessed us with five beautiful children.

My story of God's power and grace is not an isolated case there are many being healed daily as they believe on the Lord Jesus Christ and the power of His cross. Next I would like you to read the testimony of a young lady named Valerie.

A Personal Testimony from Valerie: A Victim of Sexual Abuse

We will not disclose the true name of the victim for the sake of confidence. So in this case we will attribute to her another name. Let's call her Valerie.

Valerie was sexually abused by her stepfather since she was thirteen years old. By the time I met her she was well in her middle twenties. During this time she was still in a secretive and sexually abusive relationship by her stepfather.

The abuse and mental manipulation had taken place for so long that she was too frightened to disclose it. Her parents were still married and she felt that if she would inform her mother about her stepfather's abuse she would have been greatly blamed and misunderstood. Her stepfather had warned her saying, "If you expose me I will make you look like the guilty one." She never told anyone until she met me.

One day while at work I decided to stop and talk to this young woman, because she appeared hurt within. I asked the Lord if he wanted me to talk to her in some way. I started with small conversation. One day I was burden by the Lord to intercede for this lady, as I did the Lord revealed to me that she was sexually involved with her stepfather. The next day I asked her to come to my home to visit because I had something I wanted to talk to her about.

Before she came to the house I shared with my husband what The Lord had revealed to me about her. My husband had met her several times on my job. My husband also shared that he saw the emotional pain on Valerie's face caused by her abuser. We both allowed her to visit and he and I ministered to her. She openly shared the hidden secret that was destroying her life.

That night Valerie opened up and decided to forgive her stepfather and she was released from some roots of bitterness that his torment left. We cried and prayed together and Valerie accepted Jesus Christ as her personal Savior. Time had passed and Valerie had to take her freedom to another level. She had to admit to her mother, the woman she had loved all of her life, that her husband was a sex offender.

As Valerie despised the thought of revealing this wicked secret to the woman she loved the most, all kinds of fear, anger, bitterness, and revenge began to surface in her heart. Valerie had trouble telling her mother so she asked me to help her.

Below is a poem Valerie and I composed together to explain to her mom what happened. Here is the poem.

"Mom, I can't begin to tell you"

I don't know where to begin Mom. All I know is that I love you. I never meant to hurt you. Yet, I can't tell you this without hurting you.
It's a pain I have carried for many years. A pain that had gripped me and a pain that has ripped me.
It was a secret that I had never planned, and a love affair that he put on demand.
He forced me at a young and tender age out of his sexual desire and deceptive rage.
It went on for years in the dark of the night,

While you were asleep I felt fearful and tight.
He took advantage of me so young and so tender,
You didn't know he was a sex offender.
He molested and he stripped me,
Not just of my womanhood, but of my virginity.
Whispering words of deception and lies,
Justifying incest in his lustful eyes,
Forcing me to keep a covenant and hide,
Taking me for all kinds of sexual rides,
He made me swear that I would not tell
He threatened as if he were a demon from hell.
This abuse continued for many years
Through much deception, tears, and fears,
Now that I am grown he continues this abuse,
He says if I tell that I will lose.
I can no longer keep this a secret, I am hurting and in pain, and in need of much treatment.
Mom, please keep him away. I have tried many times
He continues to follow me with his passionate bribes.
I went away to separate myself from him
He keeps coming as he did in the beginning.
He keeps saying put these things on and fill my desire
You're the young woman that has set my heart on fire.
He's sick in his mind and I won't submit any more,
I feel like a slut and a sexually abused whore.
He abuse me since I was thirteen years old,
He has always threatened me if I ever told.
Please forgive me Mom I could not tell you then,
I was afraid of this man I am now and was then.
You married him, and you didn't know,
He was a sex offender, but it didn't show.
He needs to be put away, some how and some way,
Not tomorrow MOM but today!
Please don't blame me I was too oppressed to know better,
But, since I have received Jesus in my heart, I feel I can now write you this poetic letter.
Love, Valerie

Valerie never got a chance to tell the poem to her mom, because by the time she reached her mom her sister reached her first. Valerie found out that her sister confessed to their mom that she too had been violated and sexually molested by their stepfather.

Although Valerie's sister reached her mother first Valerie's mother was sure to believe her story now. She confessed to her mom shortly after her sister did. Her mother was overwhelmed with the news and extremely angry in feeling betrayed; she immediately informed the police.

The police could do very little about the testimony of abuse, because they claimed that too many years had gone past and that they could not prove the abuse.

Valerie and her mom continue to build on a loving and forgiving relationship. Valerie's mom is no longer with her stepfather their divorce is anticipated.

The next lessons

If you are seeking sexual wholeness these next lessons include several teachings that have healed me. These teachings will instruct you through the word of God and offer some comfort as well as keys to your deliverance. I hope my testimony and Valerie's testimony of God's delivering power will encourage you to seek God for your own sexual healing and wholeness.

Sexual Sin Rooted in Idolatry

Romans 1:25-27, KJV: 25Who changed the truth of God into a lie, and worshipped and served the creature more than the Creator, who is blessed forever. Amen. 26For this cause God gave them up unto vile affections: for even their women did change the natural use into that which is against nature: 27And likewise also the men, leaving the natural use of the woman, burned in their lust one toward another; men with men working that which is unseemly, and receiving in themselves that recompense of their error which was meet.

Let's look at a few examples; In Genesis 32:1-4, the Israelites were notorious for committing rebellious acts. One specific rebellious act was worship of the golden calf idol. Their rebellion spread through the whole nation of Israel including their wives and children. The Bible declares, "The people ate and drank and rose up to play" (Ex 32:6). The Israelites participated in all types of debauchery and reveling, because of the reverence they had for the golden calf. "They changed the truth of God into the lie and worshipped and served the creature more than the creator." In 2 Kings 21:21-24, King Amon practiced the same generational sin of idolatry, as did his father Manasseh. Amon's recompense was death see (2 Kings 21:23).

In Genesis 19:5, we see Lot, Abraham's nephew in Sodom. The men of Sodom who were perverted and homosexual approached him. "They changed the natural use of that which was against nature." They tried to force their way into Lot's home and refused his request to take his daughters to have sex with instead of him.

In Genesis 19:15, the angels were sent to take Lot and his family out of Sodom because God was going to destroy that city. Lot's family had grown use to the customs and idol worship of the people of that city, as a result we see in Genesis 19:31-38 that his daughters had become just as perverted in their thinking as those of Sodom.

The Bible says remember Lot's wife. Why? She looked back and became a pillar of salt (Gen 19:26). His wife looked back because she lusted to go back to the wicked life of Sodom. Lot's family came out of Sodom but Sodom never came out of them.

His daughters plotted to get their father drunk and then have sex with him (Gen 19:32-33). The daughters got pregnant and Lot's children were of the seed of incest (Gen 19:36). Lot's children by his daughter were the Fathers of the Ammonites and Moabites that were enemies and constantly at war against the children Israel (2 Chron 27:5, 2 Kings 3:18).

In like manner, the things that possessed us or our children will constantly fight against us from generation to generation. These examples and many more are written in the word of God to warn us (1 Cor 10:6; 11, NIV). The scriptures reveal that idol worship is one of the main sources Satan uses to open the door for homosexual, perverted, and incestuous practices. Why are idols open doors?

Because "behind every idol is a demon" (1 Cor 10:20). In like manner, I was told that my family's sexual sin had its origin in Indian tradition. My grandfather was full-blooded Indian and believed in sexual perversion as part of his evil beliefs and superstitious practices. God forbade such homosexual and incestuous practices in the laws of Moses in Leviticus Chapter 18.

Worshiping idols is not only worshiping man made images like gold, stones, wood, but can also be defined as human worship (Romans 1:23). If you overly adore humans and their body parts by viewing (pornography) naked sexual pictures, or (voyeurism) live naked persons having sex you will be given over to a rejected state of mind. If you adore humans and their bodies, or anything of perverted sexual origin-like naked idols or perverted artwork, you will eventually end up rejecting what is true and proper and accepting what is homosexual or perverted.

Let us recapitulate on (Rom 1:28) it says, "they did not retain God in their knowledge so God gave then over to reprobate or rejected mind to do those that are not convenient." This scripture reveals much. Not only will those idolaters and homosexuals that refuse to acknowledge God be given over to a rejected mind; they will also do the things that are not convenient. The word convenient here means appropriate, proper or fit. Homosexuals are not fit for one another. They do not have the right sexual parts for one another; their parts do not fit. The fact that they are having sex with the wrong parts is proof of their already judged state as I stated before.

Jesus fills that Empty Place

Many people have been molested, but have no desire to be gay, or sexually perverted. Many who were molested may not realize their need for inner healing at first, but could later realize they were affected in some way. If you were molested you may have made the choice to, or, not to become like those who offended you. Either way there is still a need for emotional healing. A healing only Jesus can bring, as He gives you His loving touch, and takes the place of those sinful desires and fills the lack of love.

Are you seeking affection from the same sex? Jesus will take the place of your natural parents giving you comfort, assurance, affirmation and instruction. God understands your need to be needed, and wanted, by the same sex - a mother or father, and your desire to be attractive and accepted by them. But God forbids you to lust for or become sexual with them. "They burn or are inflamed in their lust one towards another." This perverted burning lust is the result of a reprobate mind, or a rejected mind (Romans 1:27; 28). When I had rejected Christ during my teen years I had rejected what was true and right.

Searching for love and affirmation in all the wrong places was and is true for many of us, especially those suffering from the lack of a parent's love. Maybe you are in need of a loving father and/or mother. Maybe you just need to be loved. Perhaps you are looking for identity. Whatever your search is, you need Jesus Christ and a new spiritual family.

Jesus has given us a new family. God is our spiritual Father, Jesus is our Lord and Elder Brother (Heb 2:12), the church is our mother (Gal 4:26), and the saints are our brothers and sisters. Pastors and other spiritual leaders are our spiritual parents. Jesus is also a healer to all that accept Him.

Jesus as My Lord

Jesus Christ is the way, truth and the life (John 14:6). He is the way unto God and the way out of an inappropriate thing. I invited

Him into my heart over sixteen years ago and never looked back. God destroyed Lot's wife because she looked back at the perversion she came out of (Genesis 19:26).

If you are suffering from the torment and bondage of sexual sins give your life to Jesus Christ today. God the Father and the Lord Jesus has healed, cleaned, and washed me on the inside. They have taken away the filth and stench of that once polluted and perverted lifestyle. I cried many times in appreciation to Jesus because God the Father gave me another chance to live life. I was totally set free from the practice of all types of drugs and sexual sins after receiving Christ in my heart sixteen years ago.

I am happily married with the man God has given me. As a young woman walking down the isle I thought, "Would he marry me if he knew I practiced perverted sex?" "What does he see in me anyway for him to want to be my husband?" I felt I was blessed to have someone like him. Thoughts flowed over my mind I began to pray, "Lord please cleanse me from my defilement." On the way down the isle I wept wishing I had saved myself for my husband.

God allowed me to see how precious marriage is and how sex is to be confined to the covenant of marriage, and reserved for that one special person. Thank God that there is healing and deliverance in the blood of Jesus Christ. Confess and believe in the Lord. Romans 10:9 states, "That if thou shall confess with thy mouth the Lord Jesus, and shall believe in your heart that God hath raised him from the dead, thou shall be saved [meaning delivered]."

The Healing Process

#1 Mind & Emotions: It took years for me to heal emotionally. I stopped practicing sexual immorality instantly after accepting Christ, but there were still times I would have bad dreams from all of the pornography I had seen. However, God was at work and my mental deliverance came as I meditated on his word and applied his word like ointment on a wound. The past memories would still taunt me, but I would speak the word of God and Satan had to obey.

I would use the verse in 2 Corinthians 10:5, "Casting down imaginations and every high thing that exalt itself against the knowledge of God bringing into captivity every thought to the obedience of Christ." After you ask Christ into your heart you still have to fight to gain victory over your thought life. This verse in Corinthians is powerful and just the right dose of medicine for your mind.

#2 Opening up: The first major step towards my healing took place when my husband and I had an intimate talk one year after we were married. During which time we opened up to one another and discussed everything concerning our immorality. As a result of the conversation we both learned to cry, forgive, and accept one another.

#3 Studying the Word: One day at a time I began to be restored. I read the Bible as much as I ate food. Job said, "I have esteemed the words of his mouth more than my necessary food" (Job 23:12). Jesus also said, "Man shall not live by bread alone, but by every word that proceeded out of the mouth of God (Matt 4:4). David said, "Thy word have I hid in my heart, that I might not sin against thee" (Ps 119:11). These scriptures are good healing for any soul. God's word is His promises to us. Surely He will perform what He says. If He says He is "Jehovah Raphah" know He is the Lord that heals, repairs, stitches, and makes you whole. The inner healing will come as you pray.

 # 4 Much Prayer: Jesus taught to him that was forgiven from "many" sins, loved the "much" (Luke 7:44-47). I always prayed from the beginning of my salvation. I showed "much" love to God for the "many" sins I was forgiven. I had to cry for total deliverance. I was filled with the Holy Spirit three months after I was saved and sought God with my whole heart. Jesus said, "Ask and it shall be given you; seek, and ye shall find; knock, and it shall be opened unto you" (Luke 11:9). For true healing you have to "ask," "seek," and "knock" in order to get all that God has for you. So instead of burning for sex I have a healthy passion for God. I have a passion in seeking His will for my life.

 # 5 Fasting: Jesus said, "Man shall not live by bread alone, but by every word that proceeds out of the mouth of God." Fasting should be a regular practice if you are to become totally delivered from your past lifestyle. Jesus fasted, so did Paul, Daniel, Moses, The Apostles, Anna the Prophetess and so many more. Fasting helps you to focus on your relationship with God and helps you to overcome the desires of the flesh. As you grow in grace and in the knowledge of God, make fasting a regular practice and you will kill the desire to go back into what God delivered you out of.

Recommendation

I recommend that all Christians set a time of personal prayer and fasting, attend prayer service at their local church, spend time studying God's word, and plenty of time fellowshipping with true saints. This will aid as God begins the healing process.

Can occult related sex be healed?

Many people knowingly or unknowingly get involved in occult practices and end up totally confused within. For many of them there is much need for deliverance and healing from sexual immorality, but before God can do anything for them they need to pray and renounce the devil and all his works.

No matter what you may have indulged in, God can and will forgive and heal all perversion regardless of its origin. The Bible says God is "not willing that any should perish, but that all should come to repentance (2Peter 3:9)." There is only one sin that cannot be forgiven that is blasphemy of the Holy Spirit (Matt 12:31-32). Jesus addressed this to those who call what God is doing is of the devil or evil. If you blaspheme Jesus through ignorance he will forgive you. But if you do that towards the Holy Spirit who is the spirit of grace you cannot be forgiven.

If you are an occult worshipper stop! You are on the roadway to hell. Come to the cross of Christ and find healing, peace, and forgiveness. Satan does not care about you. He will use you and destroy you. He is a liar and the father of lies (John 8:44). Jesus died on the cross just for you and me. The Bible states that all have sinned and come short of the glory of God (Romans 3:23). The Bible says, "There is none righteous, no, not one" (Romans 3:10). Come and get covered and washed in the holy blood of the lamb Jesus Christ (Revelation 1:5). This is your day and God has not forgotten about you. He will be a father to you and love you in a pure and clean way.

He has a purpose for your life and Satan has no part in it. You belong to God. He made you in his image and not in the imagination of the father of lies. Satan's going to the lake of fire please do not choose to go with him. Jesus said that hell was prepared for the devil and his angels (Matt 23:41), not human beings. Many are going to hell, because they choose to go. Choose this day for your deliverance.

Lesson #1: Secret Sins are Generational

Romans 5:19, KJV: For as by **one man's** disobedience **many** were made sinners, so by the **obedience of one** shall **many** be made righteous.

I spoke of the root of generational curses and evil influences earlier under the subtitle "Sexual Sins are rooted in Idolatry". In this lesson I would like to explain that root of influence further. Adam's "disobedience" caused "many" or should I say generations to sin. Sometimes as parents we think that we can sin and get away with it. Later on we find the same sins present in the lives of our children. What we thought we were doing in clandestine was indeed revealed in some mysterious way to our children. In a way we could not control. If we had known they were receiving sensations from our perverted lifestyles we would have tried to stop it from happening.

Whenever we sin in secret (so we think), we later realize it was not a secret at all. God has ways of telling on us through our behavior, someone else's mouth, or some situation. He does this in hope that we would repent. The word says, "Some men's sins are open beforehand, going before to judgment; and some men they follow after" (I Timothy 5:24). What we do will be obvious to others who "follow" behind us (next generation). These sins can judge us now, or our children later.

Unless our children and we are taught differently through God's word, and receive salvation through the blood of Jesus, children will follow the path of their parents' right or wrong behaviors. This verse could also be interpreted, as the sins of the parents will "follow after" them, meaning the parents. It may appear generational sins are not following you or your children, but in secret they could be.

What evil we practice, can and will, effect and defile our children. On the other hand, what they choose to do will determine whether or not the secrets sins of their forefathers proceed.

For Our Example

Look at how these parents' sins followed their children. In the Old Testament the idolatrous sin of Manasseh spread to his son Amon. The wicked sins of Lot's daughters spread to their children Moab and Ammon. These two men and their children were an idolatrous people. In light of this let us strongly consider 2 Samuel Chapters 11 & 12.

In 2 Samuel 11, David lusted for a married woman named Bathsheba, and committed murder by killing her husband Uriah. David and Bathsheba had to pay the penalty for their adulterous and wicked sin, by the death of their child. The child was the seed of their adulterous relationship (2 Sam 12:14 &18). In 2 Samuel 12, here is some of the word that the Lord declared to David through Nathan the Prophet. He said to David, "That the sword would never depart from his house," "that God would raise evil up against his house," and that what David had done in secret God "would do this thing in front of all of Israel."

David's Sins Followed

David's sons Amnon and Absalom followed the sins of their father. Amnon committed incest by raping his sister, Tamar. He did as his father David had done by forcing himself upon a woman. David and his son Amnon both took a woman who did not belong to them.

David's other son Absalom found out about his brother raping his sister (2 Sam 13:20), and killed his brother. He killed as his father had killed. What was the cause of these generational curses? The sins of the father followed the sons. David killed a man, took his wife and committed adultery with her. God judged David through the prophet Nathan and said that his children or household would suffer because of his wicked sins.

Repent of Your Secret Sins

In order for sin not to proceed, it is important to tell your children the truth about what you have done and are doing. This can help expose the sin and help them to choose the right way if they desire. Receiving salvation by repenting and changing your lifestyle will destroy the operation of every secret sin.

If parents or grandparents insist on continuing in their secret sins, it can lead to secret sinfulness in their children or grandchildren. The next generation may not perceive that their desire to do the same things came from a secret (unknown to the children) sinful lifestyle in their ancestors. Our parents may not recognize why their children or grandchildren are behaving in strange ways. Many parents and grandparents fail to recognize that their sins are passing on to the next generation. Why? Many of them were convinced that they did a good job of hiding their sins. David was convinced until the prophet came. Many of us will continue to hide our sin until we meet the Prophet Jesus who will tell us all we have ever done (John 4:17-18, 29).

Secret Sins are Known to God

Genesis 3:6: "And when the woman saw that the tree was good for food, and that it was pleasant to the eyes, and a tree to be desired to make one wise, **she took of the fruit thereof, and did eat, and gave also unto her husband with her; and he did eat.**"

We know that Adam and Eve consented to disregard the command of God. What they thought was a secret was not concealed at all (Genesis 3:8). God knew before hand that they would falter. He then made provision for them (Genesis 3:21).

However, as we look deeper into Genesis 3:6, we understand that the desire to have one piece of forbidden fruit led to generations of secret sinfulness and wickedness (Romans 5:9). Longing for that which is forbidden is the reason for all sin. David and his son wanted what was forbidden, so did Adam and Eve, and so did you and I. This scripture in James 1:14 with the Strong's Concordance definitions declare, "Every man is tempted (lit. tested) when he is drawn away (lit. dragged forth) of his own lust (lit. longing for that which is forbidden) and enticed (lit. entrapped)." (James 1:14)

What we think is just between us, is not just between us, but also between generations and nations. The consequences of our behavior will influence us, our children, their children, and so on. Whatever shape generations will ultimately shape nations. Satan seduced Eve, and her act was extended to all humankind.

It will take the blood of Jesus Christ today as it took the skins of animals (Genesis 3:21) to cover us. It will take the blood of Christ today to sprinkle many nations (Isaiah 52:15) as it took the blood of bulls in (Exodus 24:8) to sprinkle the people. God temporally with animal's skins covered Adam and Eve's sin, and God used the blood of bulls and goats in the Old Testament to cover sin until Christ came (Heb. 9:11-14). God knew he had to permanently cover, prevent the corruption of transgression, and destroy the consciousness of sin.

God had to send Christ the High Priest (Heb. 8:1) to give us a blood covenant, called the New Testament (Heb. 9:11-28). His covenant is a better covenant (Heb 8:6), because the blood of animals could not have washed away sin (Heb. 10:4). Christ put away sin by the sacrifice of Himself (Heb. 9:26). Sin is so destructive and corruptive we need a new spirit (Ezek. 11:19), a renewed mind (Eph. 4:23), and a new body to get rid of it (Phil 3:21). The old body had to die–the body of sin (Romans 6:6).

Secret Sins of the Body

A body of sin is a house of sin. Our body is the temple of God (1 Corinthians 6:19). We are also the "house of God" (Hebrews 3:6). Would you allow sin in your natural house? Why allow it in your spirit?

Let us compare, suppose you had a house party and there were all kinds of drugs, alcohol, foul language, violence, satanic worship, perversions, and gambling. Would you allow this in your earthly home? Would you allow this in your spiritual home? Many people would cringe at the idea of allowing such things in their homes. There are many people today that entertain these things in their homes, some openly, and some in secret.

One day, our bodies will tell on us (2 Corinthians 5:10). Housing sin in our physical or spiritual houses or temples, and hiding that sin is the reason why many feel ashamed and naked. Shame is the result of disobedience to God (Genesis 3:11). Our bodies will reveal the sin in us by our bad behavior and attitude. Jesus said that you would know the tree by the fruit it bears. What is coming out of us is a result of what we have allowed to penetrate our bodies and spirits. Satan penetrated Adam and Eve's minds with his subtlety and cause them to lose their innocence (2 Corinthians 11:3). Your innocence or purity can be restored as Christ sets you free.

Freedom from Secret Sins

In order to live a life free of secret sins or generational sins it will take a real relationship with Jesus Christ. His blood has washed and loosed us from sin (Revelation 1:5). We must heed God's voice speaking through the blood of Jesus instead of the voice of temptation (Hebrews 12:24). The voice that led Adam and Eve to sin is the voice of temptation. This is the voice that implores to the flesh to live and have its way. The Bible teaches that dust shall be the serpent's "meat" (Genesis 3:14). Adam was an earthly man made out of the dust of the earth.

For this reason whenever we submit to the desires of the flesh we become vulnerable to the serpent. Satan—the deceiver—will feed off of us and our dust or flesh will be his meat. Satan cannot consume those who live and walk in the spirit. This is a benefit for all who believe in Jesus and attain a spiritual mind. Jesus Christ is the second Adam. He was not of the earth, but "the Lord from heaven" (1 Corinthians 15:47). Therefore, all his heavenly blessings of righteousness fall on all who believe (Ephesians 1). He left heavenly heritage on earth. Therefore He "frees" us to follow His example.

Lesson #2: Healing Offences

Luke 23:34, KJV: Then said Jesus, **Father, forgive them;** for they know not what they do. And they parted his raiment, and cast lots.

On March 31, 2001, the Lord said to me, "This is the day of the healing of offences." Jesus said you should love your neighbor as you love yourself. Jesus said, "If your brother sin against you, you should forgive him not seventy times, but seventy times seven." In Genesis 4:23-34 Lamech was pleading for forgiveness for murder and asked to be forgiven seventy times seven. Let's read:

Genesis 4: 23-24, NIV:."23And Lamech said unto his wives, Adah and Zillah, Hear my voice; ye wives of Lamech, hearken unto my speech: for I have slain a man for wounding me and a young for striking me. 24If Cain shall be avenged sevenfold, truly Lamech **seventy and sevenfold.**"

We must forgive one another or those who have offended or perverted us, many times over and over regardless of how many times they sin against us.

The scripture teaches that if we bite and devour one another take heed that we are not consumed one of another (Galatians 5:15). Remember, Jesus said if you offend one of these least little ones it would be as if a millstone is about your neck and you be cast in the midst of the sea (Matthew 18:6). Proverbs says, "A brother offended is harder to win than a city with walls" (Proverbs 18:19).

The Bibles states that when Job prayed for his friends after all they had done to come against him, God then turned his captivity (Job 42:10). When you learn to pray and forgive those who offended and defiled you God will turn your captivity and begin to free you from the things that are holding you captive inside.

Love Forgives

These are the days that God is requiring a deeper walk of love especially for Christians. If others are to be saved we must first forgive one another and stop hating and slandering. Some in leadership positions are in many cases extremely guilty of slandering others. Whether you are apart of a church or outside of the church you still need to learn to forgive. If there is bitter hatred among any nation of people it is first detected in their leaders. There is a need for many people to be released from what happened in their past, or what did not happen in their past.

Many of us are just as angry for what did not happen that we had anticipated rather than what actually happened. Being angry with others and refusing to forgive is pride. This pride will eventually demand too much of others. All are guilty of wanting more out of a relationship or situation. Angry people always want, "what they want - when they want it." This attitude causes them to violate others by force, demand, and control. These demanding and manipulating ways are manifested by their bad attitudes, actions, and words.

It is time to move on and forward. It is time to get free from our need to be mad, control others, and have our own way. It is necessary that we learn to love and forgive others.

Do not isolate yourself when you are offended, instead, try healing the hurt between you and the other person. It is better to love than to hate. The word says, "Love is as strong as death" (Songs of Solomon 8:6).

We need to understand that we have to be as Jesus "was" and "is." We must become who He is, and to do as He did. His request was that we love one another as he has loved us (John 13:34). We prove our love for Him as we take up our cross and forgive offences. Love is an endurance walk. When we endure in love for His sake, and the sake of others we prove our love for Him and to Him. 1 Corinthians 13:7, teaches, "Love bears or endures all things." We show our love to God by enduring sufferings in our walk as a Christian. In addition, we show love towards others by being willing to endure their pain and suffering with them.

Learn to Love Yourself

One woman of God always puts it this way: "We are imperfect people serving a perfect God." How true this statement is. We are getting there, but we have got to start somewhere, but where? The first place to start is to love "you." You cannot love your neighbor if you do not love yourself. We have got to forgive ourselves for all we have done wrong, because that is the root of blaming or accusing others. Start with you then you can work on how you relate to others. In addition to what our Master taught about love, the word explains how to love people in 1 Corinthians 13, the "love chapter."

What Love is Not

One thing we can say is that we know what love is not. Through out the Bible there are examples of what love is not. Anything that is not love is considered hatred. We see Cain killing Abel, Goliath hating David, Tobiah hating Nehemiah, the heathen nations jealous against Israel, Jews hating Jesus, Judas's satanic betrayal of Jesus, and the list goes on.

Not only do we have biblical examples, we also remember what others have done to us. Our past is a daily reminder of what others have done to us. So, we blame them for our present wounded state of mind and being. Therefore, we are in bondage to the fear of it happening again. God said to me, "The fear of bad things happening will cause them to happen, over and over again." Thus, we know what love is not, but what is love?

What is Love?

I am reminded of God's love, because God is, what love really is. "Love is of God ... for God is love" (I John 4:7-8). God so loved the world that He gave Jesus (John 3:16). Jesus said, "I and my father are one" (John 10:30). How are they "one"? "One" in His love—Jesus loves the Father and the Father loves Him. Not for what He can do, but for who He is. I (Jesus) love Him as a person He loves me as I am. God said, "I am" to Moses. I believe this means more than, I am, or I exist. I believe it also means I am Love. I am all that you will ever need Moses. I fulfill all in all. I am everything before there was anything. I am love.

Why is My Pain Perpetual?

It is time to allow God to help us forgive and forget and subdue our sins in the depth of the sea as not to remember our sin any more (Micah 7:19). The day of offense is over. Should the days of over past sufferings continue? And our pains linger from day to day, months to months, and year to year? As the Prophet said, "Why is my pain perpetual, and my wound incurable, which refuses to be healed" (Jeremiah 15:18)?

Unresolved and unhealed offenses can cause us never to be healed. These wounds then infect others. Oh, what pain as we insist to persist in un-forgiveness. Are we hurting others? Or are we really hurting ourselves? Is someone putting a stumbling block in our way? Or is un-forgiveness putting a stumbling block in our way.

Remember what Jesus said about the man who would not forgive the man that owed him money – his boss forgave him, but he would not forgive his servant (Matthew 18). Jesus said, "Settle matters quickly with your adversary who is taking you to court. Do it while you are still with him on the way, or he may hand you over to the judge, and the judge may hand you over to the officer, and you may be thrown into prison" (Matthew 5:25, NIV). What am I saying, there is a penalty to pay and that is spiritual imprisonment for those who choose not to forgive—read all of Matthew 18 again. The choice is yours. But the choice is simple all you have to do is let it go. The definition for forgive means to release, so release it and let it go.

What is Bitterness?

God said to me, "Bitterness is a deep seated attitude of unforgiveness." It is that point where unresolved offenses can turn into a stony heart. We believe we have a right to be mad and hold people at gunpoint, or throw them in jail. God alone handles offenders—"For we know him that hath said, vengeance belongs unto me, I will recompense, saith the Lord. And again, The Lord shall judge his people" (Hebrews 10:30). He will deal with your enemies or those who oppose you.

Bitterness and rebellion are coupled together. The scripture teaches, "Rebellion is as the sin of witchcraft" (I Samuel 1:23). What did God mean by that? The word rebellion is translated bitterness (Hebrew definition) in this verse. So it can read bitterness is as the sin of witchcraft. Why? Because witches practice ways to get even with their enemies and deliberately harm them. The Bible says, "Love does not work ill or harm to his neighbors." Have you ever noticed in the word kill is the word ill? Yet these people work harm or ill. If you are bitter you are harming those who you refuse to forgive.

The Spirit of Offense

Once a person is offended there is anger towards the person or persons who offended them. Remember as long as you remain angry with your offender that anger is controlling your mind, will, emotions, and actions. Many times there is a strong desire for the offended person to retaliate and to stay bitter. Let us see how this transfer works: Once an offender's bitter words and retaliatory ways penetrate the heart, it can become fuel to ignite controlling or manipulating ways within the heart of the person hurt influencing them to get back or even. The offended or hurt individual could likely retaliate on the one who offended them, or possibly someone else. The evil spirits of hurt and offense can influence a person's thoughts by telling them "Someone must pay for their hurt and pain someone is the reason for their suffering."

Suffering

Sometimes I wonder will it ever be over,
There must be a purpose for it,
I can not cry or complain because I understand there is a reason,
I must bear it and joy anyway because I perceive,
It will not always be this way,
I must keep enduring until the season is up,
The time I no longer have to suffer.
By Judith V. Peart

Do not allow bitter feelings to remain in your heart. Forgive and forget about those things that have offended you. Your failure to do so will hinder your relationship with God, and your ability to form long and healthy relationships. There is a way out of your bitter pain. It is called forgiveness and the love of God. God will help you to forgive others.

Forgiveness and Love

First we must forgive "as God for Christ sake has forgiven us" (Ephesians 4:32). We were not always right; God and perhaps many others have forgiven us. How much more should we forgive others? We all have sinned; and, we all have come short of the glory of God (Romans 3:23). Release and you will be released. Unforgiveness, as Jesus described, is like the man choking the other man (not releasing him) in a forceful effort to get back what was his (Matthew 18). When you release the evil thoughts in your mind that you have towards others God's blessings, grace, and forgiveness will be released to you. This reminds me of the scripture in Luke: "Give and it shall be given." As you give to God he will give back to you. This principle does not only work for money, but can play an enormous role in forgiving others. If you forgive others they will forgive you.

Love is the major factor if we are to be healed from offenses. God said to me, "Love is the power to forgive and forget over and over again." So once we forgive, we need the assistance from God not to remember and throw it back at the person again and again. Loving them regardless of what they have done. In this we see the perfect love of a perfect God. We must forgive and love because He first forgave us our trespasses and sins.

God First Forgave Us

Ephesians 2:1-5, NIV: ¹As for you, you were dead in your transgressions and sins, ² in which you used to live when you followed the ways of this world and of the ruler of the kingdom of the air, the spirit who is now at work in those who are disobedient. ³ All of us also lived among them at one time, gratifying the cravings of our sinful nature and following its desires and thoughts. Like the rest, we were by nature objects of wrath. ⁴ But because of his great love for us, God, who is rich in mercy, ⁵ made us alive with Christ even when we were dead in transgressions--it is by **grace** you have been saved.

So, we see in these verses our sinful state. What did Paul emphasize while writing this letter to the church at Ephesus? Let us note what we were:

1. We were dead in trespasses and sins
2. We followed the ways of the world
3. We followed "the ruler of the kingdom of the air", or "the prince of the power of the air" (Eph 1:2, KJV)
4. We once lived among the world gratifying the cravings of our sinful nature
5. Following the thoughts and desires of the sinful nature
6. We were objects of wrath

Regardless of all we had done, God was rich in mercy and had a great love for us. How much more should we love one another? We were buried in trespasses it was our grave. But, God made us alive with Christ by raising us from the dead (Romans 6). He also placed us with Himself: "And God raised us up with Christ and seated us with him in the heavenly realms in Christ Jesus" (Ephesians 2:6).

Our past lifestyle deserved death, we were in death and it produced death. We were buried in our sins, but God loved us so much He raised Christ from the dead and when He did that He raised us up with Jesus (See Romans 6). So we are no longer dead but alive. Alive in Him, Praise God!! Death has no more dominion over us, because when Jesus got up He broke the power of transgression, which was the grave that was holding us. Not only were we raised up with Him now! He placed us somewhere. Where? He placed us in heavenly places in Christ Jesus. So the earth is no longer where we sit. If that is true then the desires of the flesh named in (Galatians 5:19-21) cannot rule us. Once the desires of the flesh are put to death we can learn to receive God's love and forgiveness. When we receive His love we will learn to love others.

Prayer

Dear Heavenly Father, help me to forgive those that have offended me and may they forgive me. I deserved death for my sins and you forgave me how much more should I forgive others? Lord, I admit I am bitter towards many that have hurt, defiled, abused, accused, and molested me. Please remove all bitter feelings through the blood of the cross of Christ.
Take out the root of bitterness and plant the root of your love in my heart. I desire to be free from my past hurts so I can move on in life, and be all you have planned for me to be. Help me to release the hold I have on others. When I do I know you will release the hold Satan has on me. Lord I repent for holding things against others.

I release that hold and I now pray for the individuals with whom I am angry. Lord I now forgive them. Satan I take authority over you in Jesus' name. You no longer have power over me. I have given my life to Jesus and you are no longer my Lord. I command you spirit of bitterness and un-forgiveness to leave me. I will forgive as the Lord has instructed me. I am determined to be free. Thank you Lord Jesus, thank you Heavenly Father for releasing me now by the power of the Holy Spirit. Amen.

Prophetic Word: The God That Causes All Things to Be

God will take away your past and cause you to be or become something great in Him. God took Abraham and caused him to become great. It takes time and is done through a process. One day God spoke to my heart about His ability to change people into what He wants them to be. I hope you enjoy this prophetic word as much as I did when I received it.

Spoken December 7, 1999

The God that causes all things to be causes all things to become. He causes all things that are to come and follow him. People like how things look after they are clean, but no one likes how things look when they are dirty. People like to throw away things that are dirty not realizing that all they need is to be cleaned up.

Anything dirty can become clean and can become as good as brand new. Never despise what is dirty knowing that it (you) can be cleaned up. Anything old can become new, and anything dirty can become clean, because "God" causes all things that be, to become.

Become is a change word, a process, a transformation, a making and a change. Becoming is a birth word. Anything that becomes is born by change and formation of a process.

The seed becomes a tree.
The child becomes a man.
The old become new
The weak become strong.
The dead become alive
The bound become free.
The evil can become good.

Become is a miracle word. It is the process of a supernatural change. It is the change of something natural by someone supernatural. The darkness became light--"Let there be light"(Genesis 1). God draws to things that are not right to make them right, things that are dark to make them light.

The fisherman becomes a fisher of men. God draws to people that He will be able to change. Abraham became a father of many nations. Became denotes something that was not, but became what it was suppose to be. God does not care what we used to be, but that we become what we are suppose to be.

Become denotes something that exists. "I will be what I will be." It is necessary that the be's become and come into existence not just to the natural life but also to the spiritual life.

Those that be become, and say what they are to be.
Let the weak say I am strong, and let the poor say I am rich.
Those that be, will become,
By He that be, and will say what they will be.
Those that be, by He that be,
See what be, hears what be,
And will fulfill their Destiny.

We can all change and become all that God has destined for us. Our past is just that a past. Now God has a glorious future for those that will receive His son, Christ Jesus the Lord. Before we can receive Christ and become all that we are destined to be, we must pray and cry out of the depths of our hearts to God.

Lesson #3: Out of the Depths we Cry

Psalms 130:1, NASB: Out of the **depths** I have cried to you, O Lord.

It is out of the depths not just physical pain and suffering, but spiritual pain that we cry. In order for our hearts to turn to God fully we have to cry inwardly out of our inner most being. These cries within are our prayers to God.

It is in these cries that God will purge our sins and hurts past and present. Years ago one of my spiritual mothers use to say, every once in a while you need a good cry. I know it is true because as we pray and cry out to God He cleanses our soul from the lowest place.

The Lowest Place

Psalms 88:6, NASB: You have put me in the **lowest pit**, in dark places in the depths.

As we couple these verses Psalms 130:1 and Psalms 88:6, we see that the depths are compared to the lowest place or the pit; and it is in this place we cry. In Psalms 88:1 the word says, "O, Lord the God of my salvation I have cried out by day and in the night before you." Therefore, we see that it was in the depth, this lowest place that the writer of this Psalm cried. His life had been drawn to Sheol and his soul had enough troubles (Ps. 88:3). Why do we have to get to the point of "enough trouble" where it feels like hell before we cry out to God? Sometimes it takes "hell" to get us to come to God and we still struggle.

The Struggle

Genesis 32:24-25, NASB: 24 Then Jacob was left alone, and a man wrestled with him until **daybreak (lit., ascending of the dawn).** 25When he saw that he had not prevailed against him, he touched the socket of his thigh; so the socket of Jacob's thigh was dislocated while he **wrestled** with him.

Before we can change our ways we need to meet the one who can change us and turn us around. It is only when we are left alone and realizes there is no one else to face but God. When Jacob wrestled with the angel, he was really wrestling with God. He had to meet God face-to-face as Moses did. The New American Standard Bible translates that word as "daybreak," but the King James translates it as the "breaking of the day."

This is interesting because the word daybreak is defined in Strong's (#5927) as follows: To ascend, get up, climb, increase, raise, shoot forth and spring up, etc. Jacob wrestled with God—or God is wrestling with him—until he ascended up, got up, climbed up, increase, rise up, shot forth, and sprang up. Some of us need to allow God to wrestle with us until the day breaks— and there is change in our lives.

All of the definitions listed above speak of resurrection, victory, and prosperity. We may never see God's blessings if we are not willing to allow Him to wrestle with us. The Strong's Concordance #79—Hebrew Division—translates the word "wrestle" as "grapple," "wrestle." This means, a hand—to—hand struggle. God wants you alone in a hand—to—hand struggle with him. He wants you to prevail, as did Israel.

God wants you to prevail but before you do he will break your thigh (strength) and leave His mark on your will. You will never overcome in life until God breaks you. Anyone who has ever met God walks with a limp—meaning they cannot do anything without his help or support. We need God to wrestle with us "until the day breaks and the shadows of our past flee away" (Song of Solomon 2:17).

Do Not Let Him Go

Genesis 32:26b, NIV: But Jacob replied, "I will not let you go unless you bless me."

In order for God to turn us around in our lives we need to be persistent. Jacob said, "I will not let you go unless you bless me." I said to a sister in our local church, "Do not let go of God in prayer until He blesses you." If it takes two or three hours to press through the warfare it is worth the blessing. Jacob was determined and refused to let go of God no matter how long it took. The angel even wanted Jacob to let go. He said, "Let me go for the dawn is breaking" (Genesis 32:26a). We have to pray until the dawn comes up, until the victory is won, until we overcome, until we prosper, and until we are resurrected. One preacher in the West Indies put it this way we must "P.U.S.H"—Pray Until Something Happens.

Realizing Your Nature

Genesis 32:27, NASB Updated Version: So he said to him, "What is your **name**?" And he said, "Jacob."

In the Strong's Concordance, "name" is listed under # 8034 as "Shem." The Hebrew word "Shem" implies honor, authority, character. God was saying to Jacob what is your character, name or nature. In other words who and what are you within? Jacob's reply in verse 27 was, "Jacob". It is not until we wrestle with God face-to-face that we see our true nature.

What was Jacob's nature or name? What did it mean? Translated from the Strong's # 3290 meaning heel catcher or it is from the root word Strong's # 6117 sup planter. Webster defines sup planter as to supersede (another) esp. by force or treachery."

Jacob had to admit to the angel of God his true nature. He was guilty of "treachery" which is defined as deceiver or trickster. It is a person who does not care how he gets ahead and whom he hurts in the process.

Jacob ran long and hard. He had to finally see himself and what he had done to trick his brother Esau. It was not until he struggled with God and admitted his real nature, that God broke his strength and caused him to see himself. Then, he was able to be reconciled with his brother (Genesis 33).

God wants us to see him face-to-face. He wants to wrestle with us and break our will - causing us to see ourselves - by the real nature that is inside of us. It is only when we meet God that we learn to love as Jacob did towards Esau. He no longer wanted to be a deceiver or liar, but had learned in his experience with God to be true. When we allow God to change our character, He will give us His character or name.

A New Name

Jacob prevailed because he was willing to wrestle with God. Therefore, God gave him a new name. The angel said to him, "Your name shall no longer be Jacob, but Israel; for you have striven with God and with men and have prevailed" (Gen 32:28, NASB). In other words, Jacob, you'll no longer be a trickster or deceiver, but one that rules with God.

The Bible states, that we are established in the "present truth" (2 Peter 1:12). What is God saying prophetically through his word about your present situation? You will no longer have that old Jacob like nature. You will no longer be an adulterer, drug addict, whoremonger, liar, murder, gossiper, hater, thief, homosexual, gambler, and so on. You will be "Israel"—one that rules with God. You will no longer be opposite to Him, but working for Him.

When Jacob faced God he was at a turning point in his life. He had to face himself and go from an old name to a new name from a deceiver to a ruler with God. Are you at a turning point in your life? Turn and face God. Allow Him to give you a new name.

Jesus said in Revelation 3:12 (KJV), "I will write upon him the name of my God." So, Jesus is the one that wants to change our name or character from evil to good, darkness to light, from a deceiver to being true. We have got to allow Him to get rid of every other thing that is holding us up.

Take Away the Crutches

Once we have faced our past and have faced God we need to let go of everything we are holding on to. We have got to allow God to take away the crutches. Crutches are a false sense of support. Jacob was lame because he had to learn to let God support him. Trying to hold yourself up and all that belongs to you without God's help is a false sense of support.

Jesus will take away your false hope and replace it with real hope and faith. Your false hopes and crutches are hindrances to your deliverance. What does the word crutch mean, it means to support, prop, or stay. In order for us to really experience freedom in our lives we have to eliminate all the other things that are holding us up.

In the scripture Jesus took away a man's crutches and when He did that He took away his support system (Matthew 6:25-34). Whenever God takes away something he will give you back something better. All you have to do is ask Him (Matthew 7:7-8).

Jesus realized that people needed a heart change before they could be healed. Sometimes peoples' physical condition was a result of their spiritual and mental condition. "Which is easier, to say to the paralytic, "Your sins are forgiven; or to say, "Get up, and pick up your pallet and walk" (Mark 2:9, NASB)?

Jesus as a Prophet of God knew this man's physical state was not just physical but spiritual. The paralytic needed to know his sins were forgiven by Jesus before he could get up and walk on his own. If you read all of Mark 2, you will see that in Mark 2:10, Jesus established the truth that He had the authority to forgive sins. Note: It was in Mark 2:11 He commanded the man to take up his bed and go home.

God is a liberating God. Jesus never intended for man to be bound to anything that would give him a false support, false hope, or false promise. Our crutches of any kind will not be thrown away until we understand with faith (Hebrews 11:3a) that Jesus is the one who will support, heal, and deliver us.

Jesus brought reality to this man, but what reality did He bring? That he could be forgiven, he could take up his own bed, and that he could walk or progress in life. Our greatest blessing is that Jesus is the light of the world and that through Him we see, understand, and know the truth.

This truth is that God cares so much about us that He wants to bring light on our situation. He wants to let you know you are forgiven of all sin past, present, and future. So get up and walk out of your situation.

Tell the other man that is not your husband to pack up and go. Tell your homosexual lover you had enough and the parts just do not fit. Return to your husband and children and get up and walk home. Throw the weed and cigarettes in the trash and walk. Burn those witchcraft and porno books and walk. Leave happy hour and walk. Tell the white dust that it is a must for you to walk, not just to the place where you need to advance in life, but walk home to Jesus.

In Mark 2:5, Jesus saw the paralytic's faith along with those that carried him. He will see yours, forgive you and command you to do something by faith that will enable you to walk. Faith is an action word. The man had to first believe the words of Jesus before he could obey them. God is turning your heart towards him. Show Him that you believe by acting on his word.

If you believe God's word that says there is no other name in heaven where by men must be saved or delivered, you will believe and say that in that name I am throwing away my alcohol bottles and drugs. In that name I will stop sleeping around with Tom, Jim, and Harry. By your act of faith, God will help support you in your deliverance. He will strengthen you when you consider going back.

Even if you slip and go back to some things He is faithful to forgive and cleanse you (I John). Be persistent in your deliverance knock a little harder (Luke 11:8).

I Have No Man

John 5:7, (NASB) Updated Version: The sick man answered Him, "Sir, **I have no man** to put me into the pool when the water is stirred up, but while I am coming, another steps down before me."

How many times have we all felt like this man? "I have nobody," "I have no man to help me." Oh! How pitiful we must sound. In all my weaknesses I may easily say, "I have no one to help finance this book." I choose to walk in faith and say God will help me! Because I seek not to do my own will, but the will of the one who sent me, and I will finish His work. The man at the pool believed and was healed. God was his helper (John 5:8-9).

Inner Crutches

It is necessary that we give everything up to God. The sins that we practice are only a manifestation of what is stored within our hearts. The things we deal with the most are the things within us. Pride is an inner crutch that we use to support our exalted way of thinking, to put down others and prop ourselves up. Pride is a "self" set ideology that is supported by a false and conceited form of thinking.

For some it may be jealousy, which is an attitude that lies and tells us that someone else is seeking what belongs to us, or possess what should be rightfully ours. So we get angry and become indifferent towards the person.

It may be the hurt and pain of the past that we use as a constant excuse because the enemy has filled our minds with lies, fears, and bitter resentment. Regardless of what your inner crutches or wounds are, throw them away in Jesus' name and decide to walk in humility, forgiveness, and healing.

Lesson #4: Humility and Forgiveness

2 Chronicles 7:14 KJV: If my people, which are called by my name, shall humble themselves, and pray, and seek my face, and turn from their wicked ways; then will I hear from heaven, and will **forgive their sin,** and will **heal** their land.

Before we can turn to God totally and be inwardly and physically healed, we need to humble ourselves and ask Him to forgive any sin. Then, we need to forgive others and ourselves. Foremost we have to acknowledge that we have sinned, and missed the mark, and confess that we are guilty for what we have done. Solomon had a revelation from God as to true humility and piousness after God powerfully appeared to him in the temple.

2 Chronicles 7:12-14, NASB, Updated Edition: [12] Then the LORD appeared to Solomon at night and said to him, "I have heard your prayer and have chosen this place for Myself as a house of sacrifice. [13] "If I shut up the heavens so that there is no rain, or if I command the locust to devour the land, or if I send pestilence among My people, [14] and My people who are called by My name **humble themselves** and pray and seek My face and turn from their wicked ways, then I will hear from heaven, will forgive their sin and will heal their land.

If you notice in verse 14, God made it clear that if you humble yourself, He will forgive your sin. So that tells me that many of us are still walking around in sin (doing wrong & thinking wrong), because we refuse to humble ourselves to God.

You may be at a turning point in your life. It may be a place of significant change. But in order for you to change your direction, you must first change your heart. Your feet will only go in the direction of your heart. You will never stop sinning until you have had a spiritual heart transplant. You need a new heart. The book of Ezekiel said, "Moreover, I will give you **a new heart** and put **a**

new spirit within you; and I will remove the heart of stone from your flesh and give you a heart of flesh" (Ezekiel 36:26, NASB Updated Edition). Humility is the key to getting a new heart. It is the key to change in your life. It is the key to forgiving and the main act that will turn you to God.

More Grace

James 4:6, NASB Updated Edition: But He gives a greater grace. Therefore it says, "God is opposed to the proud, but gives **grace** to the **humble**."

James 4:6, KJV: But he gives more grace. Wherefore he saith, God resists the proud, but gives **grace** unto the **humble**.

As we humble ourselves as Solomon did and pray for forgiveness, God will give us more grace as described in the book of James. Who is responsible for giving us this grace? Jesus Christ. "For of His fullness we have all received, and grace upon grace. For the Law was given through Moses; grace and truth were realized through Jesus Christ" (John 1:16-17, NASB Updated Edition).

So we see that grace and truth came by or was realized through Jesus Christ. Jesus is the one God the Father is using to demonstrate His grace to all mankind. The Greek word for grace is translated in the Strong's Concordance #5485 as "Charis"- meaning the divine influence upon the heart and it's reflection in the life. It also means acceptable, benefit, favor, gift, joy, liberty, pleasure, and [worthy of thanks].

As we humble ourselves and pray we will receive more grace from Jesus Christ. He will divinely influence our hearts and give us favor, benefits, joy, liberty, and pleasure. He will make us feel acceptable in Him and a sense of "worthiness" or appreciation towards Him for all He has done. Knowing that what was done was finished at the cross, and that He has set us free from darkness and the bondage of corruption because He is the Lord, Savior, and Messiah.

It is only when we understand the fullness of His grace that we will come to our knees in prayer and humility. It is by Grace or God's divine influence upon our hearts that we are saved through faith and not of ourselves, it is the gift of God (See Ephesians 2:8).

So we see that faith, grace, humility, forgiveness, and prayer are all intertwined. All of these things are necessary if we are to totally turn to God, and cry out of the depths of our heart to be changed significantly in our lives. As God humbles and breaks us we may feel like we are at the bottom. We may feel last of all and least of all.

Lesson #5: The Last will be First

Matthew 19:30, NASB Updated Edition: But many who are first will be last; and the last, first.

I attended a church banquet where our Bishop was speaking. That night God confirmed the calling on my life. God prophesied to me and said, "I have called you to be a prophetess and you will see many things in the realm of the spirit, things you have never seen." I was slain in the spirit when the Lord spoke to me in this audible voice and said, "The Last will be first." I remembered that as part of the scripture in Matthew 19:30, at the time I knew what He was saying, because I was feeling last of all the ministers in the body of Christ at that time. God was declaring that no matter how low I was feeling know that the last place will be a first place with him.

He will test us, turn us, and cause us to travail, but know that His permanent dethroning of our flesh is an actual exaltation of our spirit unto life. God is opposite to man. Our down is His up for our lives (James 1:9). God can make darkness as light to Him; He makes death turn into life. Remember the death of his son, Jesus, was a seed He planted to give us the fruit of eternal life.

There is a time of the birthing of our deliverance, elevation, and prosperity. He takes you through sufferings so you will know that it is Him and not you who exalts. You may feel least of all because He has made you a servant of all. Feeling least is a death to yourself, to your desires, and to the will of your flesh and mind. As we are willing to die for Him, He turns our hearts to Him for our good and for his pleasure.

You are Worthy

Hebrews 11:35-38, NASB, Updated Edition: 35 Women received back their dead by resurrection; and others were tortured, not accepting their release, so that they might obtain a better resurrection; 36 and others experienced mocking and scourging, yes, also chains and imprisonment. 37 They were stoned, they were sawn in two, they were tempted, they were put to death with the sword; they went about in sheepskins, in goatskins, being destitute, afflicted, ill-treated 38 (men of whom the world was not worthy), wandering in deserts and mountains and caves and holes in the ground.

You may feel last or unworthy, but know that the world is not worthy of you, because you are invaluable to God. When you die to yourself for the will of God through the persecution of your faith, as the world was not worthy to receive these patriots, the world will not be worthy to receive you.

You may feel tortured or persecuted as you endeavor to walk this Christian walk, but never prematurely "accept release out of your suffering so that you may obtain a better resurrection" (Heb 11:35). Do not try to escape from God's will and making for your life. If you endure through it all you will obtain a better resurrection or blessing.

Jesus became Last for You

Isaiah 53:3-5, KJV: 3 He is despised and rejected of men; a man of sorrows, and acquainted with grief: and we hid as it were our faces from him; he was **despised, and we esteemed him not.** 4Surely he hath borne our grieves, and carried our sorrows: yet we did esteem him stricken, smitten of God, and afflicted 5 But he was wounded for our transgressions, **he was bruised for our iniquities:** the chastisement of our peace was upon him; and with his stripes we are healed.

Isaiah 53:10, KJV: Yet it pleased the LORD to bruise him; he hath put him to grief: when thou shall make his soul an offering for sin, he shall see his seed, he shall prolong his days, and the pleasure of the LORD shall prosper in his hand.

He that was the least of all died for all and became the greatest of all. We may feel as Jesus felt despised, scorned and made vile. We may feel rejected, destitute and vacant of men as he did from his own people. We may carry sorrows, feelings of aguish, affliction and pain. We may know grief, malady, anxiety, and calamity as He did.

Let us look at Isaiah 53:10 with the definitions, "Yet it pleased the Lord to bruise Him and make Him an offering for sin why? So that Jesus could see his "seed" (us), and prolong the days of his seed, and the "pleasure" of the Lord which means that valued thing, desire, or purpose of the Lord (you are that valued thing) that will "prosper." Meaning, you will be pushed forward in his hand, power, ability, and strength of Jesus.

Even as it pleases the Lord to bruise Jesus, it pleases Him to bruise us. When you are bruised for Him, or suffer for Him, your life then becomes a sacrifice for others. As you pour out your soul unto death you will divide a portion with the great and divide the spoil with the strong (Isaiah 53:12). So in other words, as you suffer, as He did you will prosper and inherit what He did. You will spoil principalities and powers through His power working in you, and you and Christ will divide or share the spoils or rewards.

Loving Jesus More

The question is always how much do you love him? In John 21:15-17, Jesus asked Simon Peter, did he love Him "more than these" meaning the fishes. Do you love Jesus more than your occupation? Fishing was Peter's job. Do you love Jesus more than food? Fish was Peter's food. Fish was also symbolic of Peter's spiritual inheritance – souls of men. Jesus said to Peter, "follow me I will make you to become a fisher of men." Jesus told Peter He would make him—a fisher of men—but the fish was the very thing Jesus asked him did he love more than him.

The very things God told Abraham He would give him was the very thing He asked him to sacrifice. The very man God said would deliver mankind was crucified unto death. Why would God require such a thing? In all these examples these men had to sacrifice the very thing they loved. Peter his Job, Abraham his son, Jesus his life.

Why? The answer is love. The connection is a marriage (your love to God) and the result is a godly seed (an offering to God). God wants to know do you love me more than life and death. In God's marriage ceremony there is no "until death do us part," because it is in the death that we are joined to The Father and Jesus even more. Whether it is death to self, martyrdom, or the end of life we still are joined to God and Christ in our dying forever: When our love and devotion to God and Christ grows richer in depth and reality, our true devotion is really revealed in the cross we all must bear.

Counting the Cost

Luke 14:26-32: 26"If anyone comes to Me, and does not hate his own father and mother and wife and children and brothers and sisters, yes, and even his own life, he cannot be My disciple. 27"Whoever does not carry his own cross and come after Me cannot be My disciple. 28"For which one of you, when he wants to build a tower, does not first sit down and calculate the cost to see if he has enough to complete it? 29"Otherwise, when he has laid a foundation and is not able to finish, all who observe it begin to ridicule him, 30saying, "This man began to build and was not able to finish.' 31"Or what king, when he sets out to meet another king in battle, will not first sit down and consider whether he is strong enough with ten thousand men to encounter the one coming against him with twenty thousand? 32"Or else, while the other is still far away, he sends a delegation and asks for terms of peace. 33"So then, none of you can be My disciple who does not give up all his own possessions.

What was the master saying when He spoke concerning us being true disciples? He was saying we have to love less anyone who means anything to us, love less our lives and take up our cross to follow Him. He did not say we could not love them, but love them less than we love Him. He wants to be first in our lives. That is why He said seek ye first the kingdom of God and his righteousness and all these things will be added to you (See Matthew: 6 33). That is why He said in the Book of Revelation that the Church of Ephesus had left her first love (Revelation 2: 4).

There is much wisdom and revelation that we can learn behind these scriptures (Luke 14:26:32). We can learn about money management and cost estimation, but when read properly it is a story about a man who wanted to follow Jesus. The man did not count up the cost, or realize the price it would take to become such a disciple. The man did not consider what it would cost to follow Jesus; he did not allow Jesus to finish the building or plan Jesus started to build in him. Jesus is that foundation and apostles build on the foundation Jesus has already laid.

How often have we started to bear fruit and give up and quit before the harvest? The harvest is the righteous fruit the Lord would have produced through us. So how silly does it look to say one thing and do another. Get a job and then quit it. Go to school and never finish.

Jesus is saying the same thing about being a disciple. To prove this, if you look at Luke 14:26, you will see that Jesus is talking about being a disciple. Then in verse 28, He talks about building a tower. In verse 33, He goes right back to saying, "So then, none of you can be my disciple who does not give up all his own possessions."

Therefore, we can conclude that we must bear our cross, come after Him to be his disciple. Love Him more than anyone or anything else. Allow Him to finish what good work He started in us. Realize that it is going to cost us to love Him. Bearing our cross is the price we must pay because it was the price He paid for us. Forsaking all for him is losing our lives in him, for him, and to him, and that is love.

What You Leave You Receive

Mark 10:29-32, KJV: 29 And Jesus answered and said, Verily I say unto you, There is no man that hath left house, or brethren, or sisters, or father, or mother, or wife, or children, or lands, for my sake, and the gospel's, 30 But he shall receive an hundredfold now in this time, houses, and brethren, and sisters, and mothers, and children, and lands, with persecutions; and in the world to come eternal life. 31 But many that are first shall be last; and the last first.

Matthew 19:27-30, KJV: 27Then answered Peter and said unto him, Behold, we have forsaken all, and followed thee; what shall we have therefore? 28And Jesus said unto them, Verily I say unto you, That ye which have followed me, in the regeneration when the Son of man shall sit in the throne of his glory, ye also shall sit upon twelve thrones, judging the twelve tribes of Israel. 29And every one that hath forsaken houses, or brethren, or sisters, or father, or mother, or wife, or children, or lands, for my name's sake, shall receive an hundredfold, and shall inherit everlasting life. 30But many that are first shall be last; and the last shall be first.

As we read Mark 10, we see that Jesus said no man has left all. What they thought they would be losing would be restored and given back to them. Peter was instructed for this statement. Jesus told them what they thought they were going to lose by following Him they would actually regain. They would gain all of what was forsaken plus receive eternal life according to Matthew's account. This of course would be with persecution.

The other interesting thing was that Peter in Matthew 19: 27 said, "we have forsaken all and followed you what shall we have therefore?" Isn't this the question that we all ask who follow Christ, or those who may be interested in doing so? What shall we receive?

Jesus' answer was clear in Matthew 19:28, "in the regeneration when the son of man shall sit in the throne of his glory ye shall sit upon twelve thrones, judging the twelve tribes of Israel."

The promise that we inherit for our suffering and lost—in this lifetime—God will by far exceed what we could ever expect, as God allows us to sit with Jesus in his glory. The Bible declares that the suffering of this present time is not worthy to be compared to the glory that will be revealed in us (Romans 8:18).

Jesus said some powerful things to Peter. He said you will sit on thrones as Judges. You will get back houses, lands, children, father, mother, and wife. He said a hundredfold plus eternal life. All the bank stocks, mutual funds, or insurances in this world could not give us such a security and offer for our deposits or investments.

He finally said, the last will be first. He is the First and the Last, and has the power to place us first or last in his order. He may have been the least among his brethren as he walked the earth, but the least is the greatest in the kingdom of heaven and of men. Jesus became poor that we may become rich (2 Corinthians 8:9). He has inherited a rich throne of glory and now welcomes us into it (Revelation 3:21).

Lesson #6: The Throne of His Glory

Revelation 3:21, NASB, Revised Edition: He who overcomes, I will grant to him to **sit down <u>with Me</u> on My throne**, as I also overcame and sat down **<u>with My</u> Father** on His throne.

Hebrews 1:8, KJV: But unto the Son he saith, Thy throne Oh, God, is forever and ever: a scepter of righteousness is a scepter of thy kingdom.

Jesus told his disciples that they would sit on thrones as judges in the regeneration. They over came by suffering death for the gospel of Jesus Christ. So they qualified to merit this scripture in Revelation 3:21. We as Christians must overcome by physical death and the crucifying of our flesh. Only then will we rule with him in His throne.

We now know that the throne is His glory. What we want more than ever is to be with Him now and forever. Jesus prayed and asked the Father that His disciples may be with Him where He is (See John 17:24). Where is He? He is in the glory of His Father. This is where we should be experientially. Living in God's glory now is being in His presence. His presence or the throne of God's glory is in our hearts. When we pray and fellowship with the God that is within us, he rules our hearts, and his ruling power within, then flows out of us. It is as He rules us within that His Kingdom can be established in the earth.

No matter what you have suffered, or are suffering; God's ultimate plan is to get us in Him and in Jesus experientially. It is in this place where we are restored, his kingdom is established and He is glorified. This reminds me of a vision the Lord gave me.

Prophetic Vision of Heaven

May 6, 1996: I was sleep and got attacked by an evil spirit. I fought off this evil spirit by rebuking it. I said in my sleep, "Jesus has overcome you" and the dark spirit left, and immediately I went into a vision. In this vision I saw Jesus on a white horse with a sword, He ran toward this other army full of horsemen. I noticed Jesus was alone but the other army had a lot of men. As they raced towards one another and fought, I heard the loudest song any one could sing. The song declared, "He has overcome them, he has overcome them, He has overcome them ..." Loudly ringing in my ears.

As this part finished God took me upward, I ascended up in the air, and through the clouds. As I ascended up, I heard a song sang loudly, "For He is worthy, for He is worthy." The song was ringing in my ears. I saw heaven and New Jerusalem it was beautiful. The temple was gold and the streets were gold. The color of heaven was the color of the rainbow - beautiful. As I looked, it finally dawned on me that I was in heaven. I thought to myself, "this is where we will be and it had to be where Jesus is." As the vision continued, I felt like I was flying. I thought to myself, "I see why Jesus was able to go through walls and move from point to point in a split second after his resurrection." I continued upward and went through some more clouds. It seemed like I came to an end. At this end there was a mist or cloud. I knew God the Father or Jesus had to be behind there. I thought to myself, "I will finally get to lie at Jesus' feet and see Him in person." After these things, I awoke so elated I woke my husband.

Heaven is His throne and what I saw and experienced was the very reality of the presence of God. God wants us in His throne—with all of our being for all eternity. Jesus has prepared a place for us (John 14:2-3). I concluded this book in rap that I may minister to this generation.

Poetic Conclusion

I admitted that I needed sexual and emotional healing within; once I admitted it to God my healing began. My family's history was my story and it's that story the Lord had put to an end. Jesus took away the root of my sin he had to search deep within my origin.

My childhood was spent mostly sulking for the secret and hidden sins I was practicing. Alcohol and drugs was a part of my desire to forget what was happening making me a slave to my sexual sin.

Sex was an idol I was worshipping shifting the natural use of men to women. I had to try not to look back to where I had been it was time for me to get out of Sodom.

Jesus filled those empty places giving me sweet healing with his loving grace. I was looking for love in all the wrong places looking for men and women to fill the empty spaces. I was really searching for identity, but God's only remedy was on my bending knee.

I had to accept Jesus as my Lord it was at that moment I was restored. I began to feel free as Jesus healed me from my sexual immorality. I wrote this book and wanted to bring closure in this way, so you can understand the message and what I sought to say.

Repent of your secret sins and they will not proceed. If you fail to take heed God will expose your deeds. Your children may be defiled and pay the penalty, for what you thought you hid God made a reality, but if you repent God will cast your sin into the deepest sea.

Stop filling yourself with sexual debauchery your body is crying out "please stop doing this to me." I must love me as God loves me; it's only then that I can see what God created me to be. I need to cry out – out of the lowest place it's out of the depths of hell I'll feel His loving grace.

Jacob wrestled with God and refused to let go; as I do the same in your grace I will grow. Lord, please take away what I am holding on to, as I release these your love will increase in me. I may feel last Lord, but you will make me first by your holy power you will break away the curse. I must love you more and start counting up the cost you paid the price and died for the lost. What I lay down for you will only be restored - that is if I choose to please you Lord, more and more.

You took away a life of sexual sin,
Restored me and gave me a new beginning,
You took your blood and covered my old story,
Now, Lord I want to experience eternal life in your glory!
By Judith V. Peart 2002

Other Books

Donald and Judith other books may be purchased at: www.lulu.com/spotlight/depart

Poiema, by Judith Peart: A collection of poetry written by Judith Peart; and illustrations by one of her sons Jeshua David Peart.

Wisdom From Above, by Judith Peart: A biblically based booklet of quotes for practical living.

Sexual Healing, by Judith Peart, FOREWORD: "Your hearts will be touched, your feelings, and emotions challenged as you read this book ... Thank you Judith for your courage and transparency to help others as the Holy Spirit has helped you. Freely you have received. Freely you have given" (Dr. Sandra Phillips Hayden).

100 Never, by Judith Peart: Quotes to help women improve their marriage relationship.

The Lamb, by Donald Peart: This is a book that speaks to many issues concerning the Lamb of God as can be understood from the book of Revelation and other Scriptures.

Jesus' Resurrection, Our Inheritance, by Donald Peart: This book is a detailed look at the resurrection of Jesus Christ and the two phases associated with each of the four resurrections.

Sex Pleasures, By Donald Peart: This book is a detailed look at some of the vices of sexuality (apparent pleasures) that have damaged many, with the view to bring healing through the forgiveness of Jesus.

Forgiven 490, by Donald Peart w/Judith Peart: Jesus said "every sin and blasphemy shall be forgiven unto men," except for one particular blasphemy. Jesus wants to deliver all of mankind by forgiving us, and teaching us how to forgive others!

The Days of the Seventh Angel, By Donald Peart: A volume of the eschatology series that opens the mystery of God relative to the seventh angel who sounds the last trumpet.

The Torah (The Principle) of Giving, by Donald Peart: The text is a guide for those who desire to be a giver in the right way. It will release the bound from the curse of the law. Yet, the book will help the reader develop responsible giving.

The Time Came, by Donald Peart: A look at the change of the age accomplished by Jesus 2,000 years ago as it relates to the change of subsequent ages.

The Last Hour, the First Hour, the Forty-Second Generation, by Donald Peart: This book explores the book of Revelations, the book of Daniel, the Gospels as they relate to the last hour and the first hour of the ages.

Vision Real, by Donald Peart: What is real vision? Is vision animate or a real person?

The False Prophet, Alias, Another Beast V1, by Donald Peart is a comprehensive study manual that exposes "another beast," and his purpose.

"the beast," by Donald Peart: "Then the angel said to me: " 'Why are you astonished? I will explain to you the mystery of …the beast….'"

Son of Man Prophesy Against the false prophet, by Donald Peart: This volume is a comprehensive instruction booklet that prophesies against "the false prophet," which is the spirit of Antichrist.

The Many False Prophets (The Dragon's Tail), by Donald Peart: The seven headed dragon in the book of Revelation used his tail to fling. His seven heads are seven ruling angels—who dominate some so-called "elders…" His "tail" is a metaphor for the "many false prophets."

The Work of Lawlessness Revealed, by Donald Peart: a detailed look at the 2 Thessalonians 2, discussing topic like mystery of lawlessness, the man of sin who acts like God in the temple of God, etc.

When the Lord Made the Tempter, by Donald Peart: This book discusses the origin of Satan relative to Mr. and Mrs. Adam; and the binding of Satan by Jesus Christ.

Examining Doctrine, Volume 1, by Donald Peart: Jesus' vision for His Church must be reestablished for the 21st Century. How can we know if a doctrine if from God? Jesus, in His doctrine, gave the answer!

Exousia, Your God Given Authority, by Donald Peart: "Contrary to popular belief Jesus is the person in charge. Most in the Church speaks more about the devil than they do about Jesus' authority and the authority He has given to His Church."

The Numbers of God, by Donald Peart: This is a brief commentary on the importance of numbers in the Bible.

The Completions of the Ages, the Gate, the Door and the Veil, by Donald Peart: A book that looks at the change of the previous ages and the change from this age to the age to come.

Contact Information:
Crown of Glory Ministries
P.O. Box 1041 Randallstown, MD 21133
crownofglorymaryland@gmail.com
Phone: 410-905-0308